The Practical Points Concerning
BLENDING

GW00630574

Witness Lee

Living Stream Ministry
Anaheim, CA • www.lsm.org

First Edition, June 1994.

ISBN 978-0-87083-783-8

Published by

Living Stream Ministry
2431 W. La Palma Ave., Anaheim, CA 92801 U.S.A.
P. O. Box 2121, Anaheim, CA 92814 U.S.A.

Printed in the United Kingdom

22 23 24 25 26 27 / 14 13 12 11 10 9

CONTENTS

PREFACE

This book is composed of messages given by Brother Witness Lee in Anaheim, California, on May 27 through 30, 1994.

CHAPTER ONE

THE PURPOSE OF THE BLENDING

Scripture Reading: 1 Tim. 1:4b; Eph. 3:9-10; 1:10, 22-23
Hymns: #837, #840

OUTLINE

I. The eternal economy of God:
   A. To produce an organic Body to be an organism to God for His increase and expression.
   B. By God Himself becoming man that man may become God.
II. The local churches:
   A. Not the goal of God's economy.
   B. But a procedure to reach God's goal.
III. The universal Body of Christ:
   A. The blending of all the local churches in the divine life.
   B. Consummating in the New Jerusalem as the unique organism for the processed and consummated Triune God's eternal increase and expression.

Prayer: Lord, we praise You for Your eternal economy. How we thank You that You have brought us all into Your recovery. In the past years we have enjoyed Your rich mercy and Your abounding grace. Lord, we love You and we need You. We need You to the uttermost. This is why we have come here. Thank You for Your gathering. We look unto You for further and further mercy and grace. Be one spirit with us and anoint the entire congregation. Lord, sustain us. Be one with us in Your speaking. Lord, would You speak in our speaking? We trust in You. Thank You, dear Lord. Amen.

THE ETERNAL ECONOMY OF GOD

In this chapter my burden is to fellowship with you concerning the purpose of the blending. This purpose is quite mysterious. To know the purpose of the blending, we need to look into God's eternal economy. Our God, the moving and acting God, made an eternal economy in Himself for Christ in eternity past (Eph. 1:9-10; 3:9-11). In this economy as a plan, an arrangement, God decided to produce an organic Body to be His organism in life for His increase and expression. To carry this out, God Himself had to become a man that man might become God. He accomplished this by the way of union and mingling. Eventually, God and man did unite together and mingle together.

We need to receive something extraordinary from His living word. God became a man so that He could make man like Himself in life and in nature but not in His Godhead (1 John 3:2). He became such a man and lived on this earth for thirty-three and a half years to pass through and experience human life in order to set up a model of what a God-man is. After such a living, He went to the cross and accomplished an all-inclusive death, in which we were redeemed (Heb. 9:12). Then He entered into resurrection. In this resurrection He brought the redeemed man into God. When He was incarnated, He brought God into man. When He was resurrected, He brought the God-created, fallen, and then redeemed man into God, thus uplifting the redeemed man. He also brought His humanity in resurrection into divinity. In this way, the Bible tells us, He was born to be God's firstborn Son (Acts 13:33; Rom. 1:4; 8:29). Resurrection was a birth to Him. Before His incarnation He was God's only begotten Son with divinity but with no humanity. In resurrection His humanity was uplifted into His divinity, and He was born in His humanity to be God's firstborn Son. This firstborn Son of God is both divine and human.

Not only so, in His resurrection He caused all His redeemed ones to resurrect together with Him. The Bible tells us that we all were crucified with Him and resurrected with Him and in Him (2 Cor. 5:14; Gal. 2:20a; Eph. 2:6). Thus, resurrection was a great delivery in which God's firstborn Son and the millions of God's many sons were delivered in one birth. First Peter 1:3 tells us that we were all regenerated in the resurrection of Christ. When Christ resurrected with humanity, He was born to be God's firstborn Son. At the same time, we, the God-chosen and Christ-redeemed people, were all born with Him in that resurrection to be God's many sons.

Furthermore, in resurrection He became the life-giving Spirit. First Corinthians 15:45 says, "The last Adam became a life-giving Spirit." This last Adam was Christ as the last one of Adam's descendants. He became the life-giving Spirit that He might enter into those redeemed by Christ and regenerate them to make them the children of God (John 3:6; 1:12-13). This is the very intention of God's economy.

THE LOCAL CHURCHES

In addition to this, God desires to build all these regenerated children of God together as one in Christ. Thus, these dear ones should not be individual, separated, and scattered, but should be gathered together in their localities to be the local churches (Rev. 1:11). *Living the church life. Never leave the church life.*

Don't miss meetings. (occassional - ok; habitually- not

We may think that the local churches are the goal of God's *practically* economy. However, they are not the goal but the procedure God *We need to be in the procedure before we can arrive at the goal living in the* takes to reach the goal of His economy. We should not forget *church life.* that the local churches are not God's goal. Many of those who have been brought into the recovery love the local church to the uttermost, and they stress the local church very much. However, we should not think that when we enter into the local church life, we reach the goal of God's eternal economy. No, we are still far away from God's goal. Since the time of Brother Nee the local churches have become a very precious item in our Christian

Romans 12:1 ... the most reasonable service. Present your body | *Strengthen me into my inner man with power that I may choose You. Your will.*

life. Some of the saints may be disappointed when they hear that the local churches are not God's goal. Nevertheless, if we are just in the local churches and do not go on, we are far off from God's goal.

According to Ephesians 1:22-23, the goal of God's economy is the church, which is Christ's Body. Some may say that since the church is the Body of Christ and since we are in the church, we should also be in the Body. They are right doctrinally but not practically. We may speak much about the Body of Christ, but if we are asked what the Body of Christ is, we may be able to answer only that the Body of Christ is the church. We are in the church; that is a fact. But where is the reality of the Body of Christ? We have the term *the Body of Christ* and we have the doctrine of the Body of Christ, but where is the practicality and reality of the Body of Christ? Have you ever touched the practicality of the Body of Christ? Have you ever been in the reality of the Body of Christ?

We all need to consider this matter. We have the term and we have the doctrine, but practically, we do not have the reality. The purpose of the blending is to usher us all into the reality of the Body of Christ. I treasure the local churches, as you do. But I treasure the local churches because of a purpose. The local churches are the procedure to bring me into the Body of Christ. The churches are the Body, but the churches may not have the reality of the Body of Christ. Thus, we need to be in the local churches so that we can be ushered, or brought, into the reality of the Body of Christ. The purpose of blending is to usher us ~ .

THE UNIVERSAL BODY OF CHRIST

It is easy to know the church because it is visible. But to know the Body of Christ is not easy. Seventy-four years ago the Lord reached China and raised up Brother Nee. He was saved as a young student. Two years after he was saved, he put out publications to preach the gospel and teach the truth. He expounded the Scriptures in a way that shocked even the top missionaries. Brother Nee first presented us a clear view of God's salvation. The missionaries brought the gospel to China and preached it. We thank the Lord for that. But God's full salvation was never made clear as a complete spiritual thing until Brother Nee was raised up.

After presenting a clear view of God's salvation, Brother Nee went further and presented the church to us. When the missionaries went to China, they did not bring the church to the Chinese people. Instead, they brought their denominations. The Chinese believers honored the denominations because it was through the denominations that they heard the gospel and were saved. They were grateful to the denominations. All of a sudden, to their surprise a young "native boy" put out clear publications telling them what the church is and strongly declaring that all the denominations are divisions of the church, not the church itself. Thus, Brother Nee made the local churches so clear and precious to us who were attracted by the Lord to follow Him according to His Holy Scriptures. We treasured the local churches.

Later, Brother Nee brought us further to see Christ as life to us. That was sweet and precious to us. Then in 1939 he began to unveil to us the Body of Christ. We all received his ministry concerning salvation, the local churches, and Christ as life to us, but very few among us received his ministry concerning the Body of Christ. We did not reject it; we simply could not enter into it. In Brother Nee's speaking to us concerning the Body of Christ, it was as if he were playing the piano to a group of cows. At that time I heard the term *the Body of Christ* and I came to know the doctrine of the Body of Christ, but I did not see the reality of the Body of Christ. Brother Nee gave message after message from 1939 to 1940, but instead of our seeing the Body of Christ, there arose a great turmoil among us that forced Brother Nee to stop his ministry. By this you can see that to enter into the reality of the Body of Christ is not simple.

This is the reason that, although the recovery has been in the United States for more than thirty-two years, it has been only in these recent years that we have felt the need to enter into the reality of the Body of Christ. This is the purpose of the blending.

The biggest work in the Bible: is the Body.

Organic Union = joint, united with the Lord in real time.
   learn to live in another realm - in the T G.

   We need the word = to divide the soul from ~~Spirit~~ Spirit.
                      to slay the enemy.

      To be an organism: God has a way to move on the earth
      in real time.

      Christianity replaces Body with religion
                        Body   church
                        Body   church life.

         v.s. (intrinsic awareness)
      Outward → reality.
      ⊘   Not just be satisfied with outward forms.
      (even the outward practice
      is not up to speed).

      If you are on time, you are late.

      We need to make the effort.

   LS | Cor message 46
                                    and enjoyed
                                    ↓   with
   They had indwelling Spirit, sharing the Christ experienced ~~by them~~ one another.
   (PP1 In Jerusalem. No hymnal. OT. NT).

         the living
We are ~~the~~ ~~living~~ functioning members of the Body of Christ. Christ is the Head.
   many opportunities to practice to be living, functioning members of the Body of Christ.

Chapter Two

THE NEED OF THE BLENDING

Scripture Reading: 1 Cor. 10:17; 12:24
Hymns: #501, #841

OUTLINE

I. The regular procedures of the church work in the Lord's recovery today:
   A. Begetting—to have sinners saved and regenerated to become the members of Christ—1 Cor. 4:15b; Matt. 28:19.
   B. Nourishing—to feed the new believers for their growth in the divine life—1 Thes. 2:7; John 21:15, 17.
   C. Teaching—to perfect the saints that they may mature to be built—Matt. 28:20a; Eph. 4:12-16:
      1. In the local churches—Rev. 1:4a, 11.
      2. For the building up of the Body of Christ—Eph. 4:12b, 16.

II. The need of the blending for the building up of the Body of Christ:
   A. To blend all the local churches together as one, as many as possible, in the processed Triune God, the pneumatic Christ, and the consummated Spirit.
   B. The Lord blending the seven churches in Asia by writing them one epistle composed of seven epistles to each of them respectively—Rev. 1—3.
   C. The apostle blending the churches in Colossae and Laodicea by writing one epistle to each of the two churches respectively and asking them to read the two epistles reciprocally—Col. 4:16.

Prayer: Lord, we are grateful to You that You have gathered us again into Your name in the move of Your Spirit and under the cleansing of Your precious blood to come to touch You and pursue You according to Your Holy Scriptures. Lord, we tell You that we need You all the time. This morning, even the more, we ask You to come down to visit us, to touch every heart and every spirit and open up the minds of the entire congregation. Lord, anoint us; anoint our mouths to speak, and anoint our ears to hear. Give us the understanding. Open the heavens to us. Open Yourself, even open Your heart; and also open us toward You. We desire to hear Your word from Your heart. Lord, we do not like to have a doctrine or teaching in dead letters. We are not here for this. We are here for touching You deeply in the depths of Your word. We do not want to be skating on the surface; we desire to go down to the bottom to see You, to see Your heart, to see what You want today. Even today while we are in Your recovery, we want to know what Your move is. Lord, grant us the revelation. Grant us a vision. Grant us the seeing that we need. Lord, be one spirit with us in speaking and in hearing. Amen.

My burden in this chapter concerns the need of the blending. Even among us who are in the recovery, not many have the realization that we need the blending, and we need it desperately. The heavy burden in the ministry that is on my heart and in my spirit is the matter of blending. In the past three months I offered to the Lord many prayers, asking Him to do something in His recovery. At the present time there are more than sixteen hundred local churches established by the Lord in all the six major continents. I receive letters from abroad quite often telling me of the situation in different places around the globe. As I look at the whole situation of the recovery, seemingly it is quite encouraging. Apparently, the churches are going on well and are flourishing, increasing, and growing. But the more I know this and the more I feel encouraged, the deeper I am burdened. It seems that the Lord within me is saying, "Is this all that I want? Do you believe that My Body can be built up in the common situation that is among us today? Is the present situation satisfactory for Me to go on?" I feel deeply that it is not.

After I had remained in the United States and had spoken for the Lord for a little over thirteen years, we moved from Los

Angeles to Anaheim, and we changed the way of practicing the Lord's recovery somewhat. Some people say that beginning from that time, my speaking changed. They say that after the move to Anaheim, my speaking was not as powerful as in the previous thirteen years, from 1962 to 1974. However, the people who say this do not know the burden that I received from the Lord.

In the first period of my ministry in this country, I traveled to many places to hold meetings and to speak mainly on the experience and enjoyment of Christ. I agree that my ministry at that time was rich and powerful and full of impact. But when we were flourishing in Los Angeles, we felt that we needed to move to a new place, and we came to Anaheim. From that time I received a burden to change from always holding conferences to conducting semiannual trainings to get into the life-study of His Word. Although I had given message after message, still the Word, the Holy Scriptures, had not been opened up. For the long run there was the need for the opening up of the holy Word so that people could see the life in this book. Therefore, each year for the past twenty-one years I have conducted two annual trainings lasting ten days each. At the present time nearly the entire Bible has been finished; only a few books remain. If the Lord wills, perhaps by the end of 1995, we will finish the entire life-study of the Scriptures.

I have received many letters from people who appreciate all the truths that have been opened up to the church from the Life-study messages. They have reached many people on this earth. They are the riches kept in storage in the recovery. Whenever you desire to know a particular truth in Genesis, you can simply open the Life-study, and you will taste how sweet, how enlightening, how supplying, and how nourishing it is.

In approximately 1980 I began to see the truth of God's economy. To open up the entire Bible from the first page to the last is needed, but what is the central matter in the Holy Bible? This central matter is the economy of God. The economy of God is for the Body of Christ. After seeing this, I checked with myself, "Where is the Body of Christ? You have opened the Bible book by book to the saints, and there are more than sixteen hundred local churches raised up on this earth, but where is the Body? You have the churches, but where can you see the Body?" Because

Because the reality is in the spirit.

We need to exercise our spirit.

[handwritten top margin:] Cookie cut outward procedure.
~~yet~~ yet without reality.

[handwritten top right:] Overcomers are needed:
living in the reality of the Body of Christ.
Blessing comes out of Zion.
cooperate with others

[handwritten above first line:] Save us from the wandering of our soul. [Much fruit came from abiding, in genuine

of this, I became burdened. I said, "Lord, I must confess to You *[one accord?]*
and admit that although I <u>saw</u> the Body of Christ and I <u>preached</u>
and <u>taught</u> the Body of Christ for years, even <u>I myself am not</u>
<u>very much in the reality of the Body of Christ</u>." I was confess-
ing my <u>dullness</u> and <u>shortcomings</u> to the Lord concerning this
matter. Thus, the present burden has come to me. You <u>should</u>

[handwritten left margin:] Carry out Not the outward way, but in the intrinsic way

[handwritten above line:] What are you spreading?

<u>not pay so much attention to the spreading of the recovery</u>, to
<u>the increase of the churches,</u> and to the <u>good meetings of the</u>
churches. <u>You must realize that there is a great lack</u>, a shortage,
that is, <u>the reality of the Body of Christ.</u> It is for this reason
that there is a need for the blending.

REACHING THE HIGH PEAK OF ZION

[handwritten left margin:] (Prayer. Spirit. Word).
through the cross

In today's education the goal is not merely to finish elementary school and junior high school and then to graduate from
high school. The goal is to study in a university and to earn not
only a bachelor's degree but even a master's degree or a Ph.D.
After many young people finish high school, they become tired
of studying and terminate their education to get a job and make
a living. This is just like our church life. <u>To be in the church life</u>
may be likened <u>to being in high school.</u> <u>Being satisfied to be</u>
<u>merely in the church life,</u> we may say, "Praise the Lord! Halle-
lujah for the church life! How good it is!" But will this reach the

[handwritten left margin:] Be in it intrinsically.
Be a factor of life.

goal for the fulfillment of the Lord's purpose? <u>It will not</u>, just
as graduating from high school will not reach the goal of the
purpose of today's education. Today in the recovery, we need to
go on and on to <u>reach the high peak of God's economy</u>, that is,
<u>Mount Zion</u>.

Jerusalem is built on the top of a mountain. Although Jerusalem is good, it is not the peak. In Jerusalem there is a peak,
that is, Mount Zion, on which the temple was built. About one
thousand years before the building of the temple, God asked
Abraham to <u>offer his son Isaac on Mount Moriah</u>, which is another name for <u>Mount Zion</u> (Gen. 22:2; 2 Chron. 3:1). The good
situation in the recovery today is just like <u>Jerusalem</u>. However,
there is <u>no Zion</u>. In the New Testament the overcomers are
likened to Zion. In Revelation 14:1 the one hundred forty-four
thousand overcomers are not just in Jerusalem; they are on the
peak of Zion. <u>The overcomers,</u> the vital groups, are today's Zion.

[handwritten bottom margin:] We have to be intrinsically in the coordination
(uncomfortable. wanting to do in my way, natural leader and natural follower).

The reality of the VG. Not VG in name only

My burden today is to help you reach the peak of the vital groups, that is, the overcomers' Zion. Although we may have a good church life, among us there is almost no realization, no practicality, no actuality, and no reality of the Body life. This is the need in the recovery today.

THE REGULAR PROCEDURES OF THE CHURCH WORK IN THE LORD'S RECOVERY TODAY

The regular procedures of the church work in the Lord's recovery today consist of four steps: begetting, nourishing, teaching (perfecting), and building. Begetting is to have sinners saved and regenerated to become the members of Christ (1 Cor. 4:15b; Matt. 28:19); nourishing is to feed the new believers for their growth in the divine life (1 Thes. 2:7; John 21:15, 17); and teaching is to perfect the saints that they may mature to be built (Matt. 28:20a; Eph. 4:12-16). The steps of begetting, nourishing, and perfecting are all for another higher step, that is, for the building up of the Body of Christ (vv. 12b, 16) in the local churches (Rev. 1:4a, 11). However, we need to ask ourselves, "Where is such a building? Where is the Body of Christ today? Within and among the many local churches, where is the reality of the Body of Christ?" According to my observation, we cannot see the reality of the Body of Christ anywhere today.

You may argue that the church is the Body of Christ. Yes, it is; but to be in the reality of the Body of Christ is not just a matter of setting up local churches with the establishing of elders and the practice of the church life in a particular way. This is merely an arrangement, a work, a service. It is not the reality of the Body of Christ. Even though our preaching of the gospel may be very good, there may not be much reality of the Body of Christ.

In the churches today we may have many saints in "elementary school," many in "junior high school," and many in "high school," but where is the "university" that can educate people up to the standard of a "master's degree" and even to the highest standard, a "Ph.D."? Where is the "university" for the Lord's recovery? I do not mean that we should set up a seminary. But we should not pay so much attention to the mere establishing of the churches and the arranging of many outward things. These have nothing to do with the reality of the Body of Christ.

This does not mean that we should close the doors of all the local churches. That would make the situation worse. This would be like saying that since there is no possibility for us to have universities, let us forget about high school, junior high, and elementary school. That would make us primitive and backward.

The highest peak of the Lord's recovery that can really, practically, and actually carry out God's economy is for God to produce not many local churches in a physical way but an organic Body to be His organism. We all have a physical body, but our body actually is not the reality of our being. My body is me, but it is not the reality of my being. Likewise, the churches set up around the globe are a physical frame, but among the churches there may be no reality of the Body of Christ. If we are honest with ourselves, we must admit that this is our situation today. Where is the reality of the Body of Christ?

THE NEED OF THE BLENDING
FOR THE BUILDING UP OF THE BODY OF CHRIST

The thought of blending is very strong in the Bible. In the Old Testament there is a type of the blending for the fulfillment of God's economy. However, if we read the Old Testament only in letters, we will not be able to see it. This type of the blending is strongly referred to by the apostle Paul. In 1 Corinthians 10:17 Paul says, "Seeing that there is one bread, we who are many are one Body; for we all partake of the one bread." Paul's thought of the church being one bread was not his own invention; rather, it was taken from the Old Testament. The meal offering in Leviticus 2:4 consisted of cakes made of fine flour mingled with oil. Every part of the flour was mixed, or mingled, with the oil. That is blending. Paul tells us that the church is a bread, a cake, made of fine flour. This fine flour comes from wheat grains, and the wheat grains come from the one grain of wheat, which is Christ. John 12:24 says that Christ is the one grain of wheat who fell into the earth and died and grew up in resurrection to produce many grains, which are we, His believers. We are the many grains so that we may be ground into fine flour for making the cake, the bread, of the church. Here we can see the thought of blending in the Bible.

Later, in 1 Corinthians 12:24 Paul writes, "God has blended

the body together, giving more abundant honor to the member that lacked." This verse says clearly that God has blended all the believers together. But where is the blending in the recovery? We may think that the coordination in the church is the reality of the blending. However, I must tell you that even the coordination in the church is not the reality of the Body of Christ. At this point you may wonder what the reality of the Body of Christ is. This is why there is the need to set up a "university" or a "college" so that we can go on from "high school" to reach the highest peak, the reality of the Body of Christ.

THE BODY OF CHRIST BEING ABSOLUTELY IN THE RESURRECTION LIFE OF CHRIST

A great part of the believers in the local churches are still in the natural man, but to be in the reality of the Body of Christ, we need to be absolutely in the resurrection life of Christ. We do have some good coordination in the local churches. However, I would ask, "Is this kind of coordination carried out by the natural life or in resurrection?" To be in resurrection means that our natural life is crucified, and then the God-created part of our being is uplifted in resurrection to be one with Christ in resurrection. In Philippians 3:10 Paul says that we all need to be conformed to the death of Christ by the power of His resurrection. We all need to ask ourselves whether the coordination among us is by the power of Christ's resurrection or merely by our natural man.

I do not believe that everything I have done in the past thirty-two years in the United States has been in resurrection. I do not deny, and I cannot deny, that as I was carrying out the Lord's ministry, especially the ministry of life to establish the churches, some part was in resurrection, but not every part. Anything that is carried out even scripturally but in the natural life is not the reality of the Body of Christ. The Body of Christ is absolutely something in the resurrection life of Christ.

It is common today that in the local churches what we can see is mostly the "church" in its meetings, activities, works, and services. But we cannot see much of the reality of the Body of Christ in resurrection, that is, in the Spirit, in the pneumatic Christ, and in the consummated God. So there is the need for us to endeavor <u>to be absolutely in the resurrection life of Christ</u>. We need to endeavor to reach in the church life the highest peak, today's Zion, of the reality of the Body of Christ until we consummate in the New Jerusalem, including Zion. Dear saints, this is our need. <u>To have the blending</u> is <u>to meet this need.</u>

CHAPTER THREE

THE SIGNIFICANCE OF THE BLENDING

Scripture Reading: Gal. 1:4, 13-14; Phil. 3:3-8, 10; 2 Cor. 3:6
Hymns: #541, #539, #976

OUTLINE

   I. Not an organization of any nature.
  II. Not a system in any way.
 III. Not a kind of unification in the outward practices.
 IV. But an organic building of the God-men who are perfected in life as the representatives of a local church, as Zion within Jerusalem, and who live the reality of the Body of Christ.

Prayer: Lord, we trust in Your mighty name and we trust in Your prevailing blood against the enemy, against the evil one. Lord, cover us and protect us and bring us through this meeting in Your mighty name.

In this chapter we want to see the significance of the blending. We have seen that the truth of blending is in the holy Word. Hardly anyone speaks about blending because this is not only very high and deep but also very mysterious. It is not a physical matter.

THE LOCAL CHURCHES BEING THE PROCEDURE TO REACH GOD'S GOAL

When Brother Nee was raised up by the Lord, he saw the light that the local churches are needed for the Lord to take the procedure to go on to reach His goal in His economy. So he stressed the local churches very much. For seventy-two years we have all followed this revelation. We have stressed the local churches again and again.

Recently, among us there has been a kind of rebellion since 1987. One of the leading ones in this rebellion picked up the wrong teaching of G. H. Lang in his book *The Churches of God*. In this book Lang stressed the autonomy of each local church. This was an old wrong teaching by the Brethren. We knew this already. Yes, we do stress the local churches, but we do not stand for the autonomy of the local churches.

The one church is expressed in the local churches because of physical reasons. We believers are scattered on this earth, so we cannot be in one location. We have to be in many locations, so in a sense, we have to be separated by localities. But we cannot forget that the churches are the Body of Christ. Ephesians 4 says that there is one Body (v. 4). Paul says that though we are many, we are still one bread and one Body (1 Cor. 10:17).

The parts of our physical body cannot be autonomous. Is it possible that the shoulder is one autonomy, the nose is another autonomy, and the two feet are two other autonomies? If this is so, then our body becomes a divided carcass. In the same way, Christ's Body is an organic unity, and no part of His Body can be autonomous.

The British Brethren stressed very much that the seven local churches in Asia, spoken of in Revelation 2 and 3, were different, independent, and autonomous. Some even said that there is not only the local church but also the local Body. That would mean that Christ has thousands of "Bodies." Based upon the wrong teaching of the Brethren, some dissenting ones said that in Revelation 2 and 3 the seven churches are different, so seven different epistles were written to them respectively. This seems reasonable, but we need to see that in Revelation 2 and 3 the seven churches are different on the negative side. They are different in their failures, mistakes, sinful things, and wrongdoings.

In Revelation 1 the Lord showed us seven lampstands, which are the signs of seven churches. These seven lampstands are all identical in nature, in essence, in size, in type, in appearance, in color, and in function. No one could discern which lampstand is which unless you put a label on each one of them. How could you say that these seven local churches are different? The Lord rebuked them for all their differences. Yes, the Lord did write epistles to each of them respectively. But He bound these epistles together to make a total epistle, an aggregate epistle.

In the whole book of Revelation the Lord showed us that the overcomers are not of different groups. The overcomers always are one unique group. The dead overcomers are signified by the man-child in Revelation 12, and the living overcomers are signified by the firstfruits, the one hundred forty-four thousand standing on Mount Zion, in Revelation 14. These are not different groups of overcomers but one unique group.

Not only so, eventually, the book of Revelation does have a consummation. In this consummation all the seven lampstands disappear. In the first chapter we see the seven lampstands. But in the last two chapters we see only one city. Eventually, the local churches will be over. Only the Body will remain and remain forever, and this Body of Christ is the unique tabernacle as God's dwelling place on this earth, the unique bride of the Lamb (21:2-3). We all have to see this.

Therefore, we must pay much more attention to the Body of Christ than to the local churches. This does not mean that I annul the teaching of the local churches. We still need it. As a person, we have a physical frame. That is our body. But a body by itself is a carcass. A physical body needs an inner life. Today the church is the same. On the one hand, it does have a frame, a body, but this frame is not the nature, the essence, or the element of the church. Ephesians 4 tells us the church is the Body, and within this church is the Spirit, the Lord, and the Father (vv. 4-6). The Father is the source, the Lord is the element, and the Spirit is the essence of the Body. These four entities are built together.

The Body of Christ is composed first of the redeemed ones, who were born by the Spirit to be the children of the Father. They are the God-men, and they are the very Body of Christ, the framework. Built within them are the Spirit, the Lord, and the Father. All three of the Divine Trinity have been built into the redeemed, regenerated believers. So there is such a building, such a structure, constituted with humanity and divinity in the Divine Trinity. Man, the Spirit, the Lord, and the Father are built together. This is not just three-in-one. This is four-in-one. God became a man so that we, His redeemed, might become God. With Him there is the Godhead. But regardless of how much divine life and divine nature we have to be the same as God, we do not have the Godhead.

THE ULTIMATE CONSUMMATION

We need to see that there is something on this earth structured as a kind of organic constitution, which is called the Body of Christ, and this Body of Christ is the organism of the unseen God. Dear saints, this is the consummation of everything. Many things are mentioned in the Bible, but eventually, at the end of the Bible, there is only one consummation, and this consummation is the New Jerusalem. In this consummation we can see God (the Father, the Son, and the Spirit) and God's redeemed humanity. We can see Israel because the New Jerusalem bears the names of the twelve tribes representing saved Israel (Rev. 21:12). We can see the believers because the holy city bears the names of the twelve apostles representing all the New Testament believers (v. 14). The New Jerusalem is the consummation of God and man. God has constituted Himself into our humanity, and our humanity also has been constructed into His divinity. Now divinity and humanity are joined, united, mingled, and blended together.

Do we need to wait until the New Jerusalem comes before we blend? There is not such a thing. The New Jerusalem comes into existence by the blending of God with His elect, His chosen people. Even the Old Testament people such as Enoch, Noah, Abraham, Moses, David, Isaiah, and all the prophets were blended together. They were not just individual saints. They were considered by God as a nation, a corporate entity, on this earth. This corporate entity was not only incorporated with men but also incorporated with God.

Then in the New Testament we also see a marvelous blending. The Lord Jesus blended all the seven churches in Asia together by sending them one aggregate epistle. Paul blended the churches in Colossae and Laodicea by writing one epistle to each of the two churches respectively and asking them to read the two epistles reciprocally (Col. 4:16). This indicates that in the eyes of Paul those two churches were one. They both should know the same thing.

Eventually, the coming out of the divine revelation is a city, the New Jerusalem. That is the consummation of God, Enoch, Noah, Abraham, Moses, David, Isaiah, Peter, John, Paul, Darby, Watchman Nee, you, and me. The New Jerusalem is the ultimate consummation of God's eternal economy.

The Lord has opened up to us the truth of God's economy with God's dispensing. First Timothy 1:4, Ephesians 1:10, and Ephesians 3:9 all use the word *economy,* a translation of the Greek word *oikonomia.* This economy with God's dispensing will consummate in one city. When we composed our hymnal thirty years ago in 1964, I wrote a number of hymns on the New Jerusalem (*Hymns,* #971-972, 975-976, 978-980). Since 1984 I have given many messages on the New Jerusalem. The last nineteen chapters of the book entitled *God's New Testament Economy* are concerning the New Jerusalem. After my study of the Bible for the past sixty-nine years, what have I seen? I would say that I have seen the New Jerusalem. This is my vision, this is my revelation, and this is my ministry. I have been in the United States for thirty-two years, and I have published approximately four thousand messages. I have stressed the Triune God, Christ, life, the Spirit, the church, the Body, and ultimately, the New Jerusalem.

What is the significance of our blending? It is not an organization of any nature. The first stanza of *Hymns,* #541 says, "Not the law of letters, / But the Christ of life." Then stanza 4 says, "Not religion, even / Christianity, / Can fulfill God's purpose / Or economy." Our blending has nothing to do with the dead letter, any religion, or anything of Christianity. The significance of our blending is the reality of the Body of Christ. This reality is nothing but the group of God's redeemed who have all been made God, the God-men, by God. They live a life not by themselves but by another life, which is within them. This other life is the Triune God processed and consummated to enter into them and to take them as His abode, His dwelling place.

Ephesians 3:17 tells us that Christ is now making His home in our hearts. In John 14:23 the Lord said, "If anyone loves Me... My Father will love him, and We will come to him and make an abode with him." This word *make* is not a small word. To make is to build. The only way to make a home is by building. This building is not by anything physical but by the spiritual element and spiritual essence of the Divine Trinity. This building actually is a kind of organic constitution. The reality of the Body of Christ is a living by all the God-men united, joined, and constituted together with God by mingling humanity with divinity and divinity with humanity.

REJECTING OUR NATURAL LIFE
AND LIVING BY THE DIVINE LIFE WITHIN US

Now that you realize this, what should you do? Every day remember that you are a God-man. You have God living in you, making His home in you. You and He, He and you, are mingled together as one. You should not live a life by your natural life, your natural man. You and I, the old man, the natural man, have been terminated on the cross, crucified by the Lord in His death (Gal. 2:20a). We must leave our natural man on the cross. This is what it means to bear the cross. By leaving your old man on the cross, you will be conformed to the death of Christ (Phil. 3:10).

The death of Christ means that when Christ lived on this earth, He was always rejecting Himself. He told us that He never did anything by Himself, but He did everything by the Father

(John 6:57; 5:19; 4:34; 17:4; 14:10, 24; 5:30; 7:18). He had a very holy, pure human life, but He did not live that life. He put that life aside, put that life to death, and lived by the Father's life. That was a model to us. We should be the mass production of that model, the God-men who have both the human life uplifted in Christ's resurrection and the divine life. Even our human life has been uplifted in Christ's resurrection, but we should not live by that, by ourselves.

Paul says, "I am crucified with Christ; and it is no longer I who live, but it is Christ who lives in me" (Gal. 2:20a). This is not an exchange, because Paul goes on to say, "And the life which I now live in the flesh I live in faith, the faith of the Son of God" (v. 20b). Paul was a person living not by himself but by the pneumatic Christ, and this pneumatic Christ is the all-inclusive Spirit, who is the consummation of the processed and consummated Triune God. All of this is in resurrection. When you do not live by your natural life but live by the divine life within you, you are in resurrection. The issue of this is the Body of Christ. The reality of the divine life within us is the resurrection, which is the pneumatic Christ, the all-inclusive Spirit, and the processed and consummated Triune God. I hope that this brief fellowship will help us to know the significance of the blending.

CHAPTER FOUR

THE REALITY OF THE BODY OF CHRIST

(1)

Scripture Reading: Gal. 2:20; Phil. 3:10; 1:19-21a; Rom. 8:4;
John 5:30-31; 6:46, 57; 14:19-20
Hymns: #972, #976

OUTLINE

  I. The corporate living by the perfected God-men, who are genuine men but are not living by their life but by the life of the processed God, whose attributes have been expressed through their virtues.

 II. A corporate living of the conformity to the death of Christ through the power of the resurrection of Christ— Phil. 3:10.

III. The mingling living, in the eternal union, of the regenerated, transformed, and glorified tripartite God-men with the Triune God (who is the pneumatic Christ as the embodiment of the processed and consummated Triune God, who is the all-inclusive Spirit as the reality of the pneumatic Christ and the consummation of the processed Triune God) in the resurrection of Christ, of which the life-giving Spirit is the reality and which imparts the consummated God and releases the death-overcoming life into the believers.

IV. Consummating ultimately in the New Jerusalem in the new heaven and new earth as God's increase and expression for eternity.

Prayer: Lord, we worship You with all our thanks and praises that You have brought us through all these days by Your marvelous mercy and abounding grace. This morning our trust is still You. We enter into You to enjoy You as our trust while we are speaking and listening. Lord, anoint the meeting. Anoint Your speaking, Your oracle, not our speaking, through Your Spirit to reach us and to touch the depths of our being that we may be fully enlightened and unveiled by You for Your eternal economy. Lord, we need You again and again, even the more today, to be our sustaining power and our strengthening. Lord, lead us and guide us to speak with You. We do not like to do anything without You. Lord, we like to speak, to move, and to act with You. Lord, in our speaking we give all our adoration to You. You are the very God, the very Lord, the Master, and the Husband to us. Thank You, Lord. We can never thank You enough. We also ask You to cover us with Your prevailing blood.

In this chapter we come to the highest peak in God's economy—the reality of the Body of Christ. We know the term *the Body of Christ*. We may even have seen the revelation of the Body of Christ. Yet we have to admit that thus far, over the past seventy-two years, through such a long time, we can see very little of the reality of the Body of Christ within us and among us. I am speaking not of the revelation, not even of the vision, but of the reality of the Body of Christ.

This reality has nothing to do with any kind of organization or with anything that remains in the nature of organization. Also, the reality of the Body of Christ is not a system in any way, because no system is organic. The reality of the Body of Christ is absolutely and altogether organic.

THE REASON FOR DIVISIONS

Today some of the dear Christians are promoting the unification of so-called Christianity. They realize that Christians should not be divided into many denominations. Throughout my Christian life, especially in my ministry, I have been checked again and again by people. When I talked to them, even about the gospel, they would say, "Mr. Lee, what you have been saying to us is good, but there is one thing that we cannot understand. Is Christianity one? If it is, why are there so many denominations? One is called Presbyterian, another is called Southern Baptist, and another one is called Methodist. What is this? We appreciate Christianity, but we are bothered. Why do you have the Catholic Church and the Protestant churches?" I could only say to them, "At any rate, Jesus Christ is unique, real, and true. I am not preaching Christianity to you. I am preaching Jesus Christ to you. Please forget about Christianity, but receive this One, Jesus Christ." By this we can see the problem of divisions.

Then the Lord raised up the recovery. Yet what a shame that even in the recovery, we were attacked by some who were with us and who became very dissenting and divisive. What is the reason for this? Now I can tell you what the reason is. When I was with Brother Nee for twenty years, I was under him as a big umbrella, and no one attacked me. All the attacks by the dissenting ones in division went to him.

Later, I was sent out abroad. First, I worked in Taiwan and the Philippines. Every year I spent one-third of the time in the Philippines and two-thirds of the time in Taiwan for eleven years. I suffered the same thing as what I had seen with Brother Nee. I was surely expecting to have an umbrella. Instead, I have become the umbrella. All the attacks with the lies and defamation have been aimed at me.

One group of dissenting ones in the Far East said that the leading ones in the recovery had all become old and were good to be buried. They told people that they had the revelation, so they considered themselves the people of revelation, claiming that they had seen the very Christ of glory. When I heard about that, I wondered and said, "Dear ones, since you have seen the vision of Christ, you should minister what you have seen to the saints in the Lord's recovery. You don't need to condemn others by saying that they are old and ready for burial."

After I spent those eleven years in the Far East, I came to the United States. In 1977 and 1978 another trouble took place. That was a case of people who came to us with an ambition to take the lead in the recovery. I used to tell people that the recovery of the Lord is not ours, but it is the *Lord's* recovery. Whoever touches it in a negative way will suffer spiritual death. This is like the man at David's time who touched the Ark with his human hand. That one suffered death (2 Sam. 6:6-7).

Nine years later in 1987, there was another turmoil among us. During those nine years I put out many messages on life, on the economy of God, and on the dispensing of God. The dissenting ones said that Brother Lee's ministry was all right up to 1984, but from 1984 Brother Lee changed in his ministry, and this changed the nature of the recovery. So they said that they had to do something to rescue the recovery out of the change by the wrong ministry of Brother Lee. They falsely told people that I did not speak as I did in the past on life, Christ, and the Spirit, but instead I would always talk about statistics, budgets, and numbers. Actually, these ones and some who are not among them but like them took the advantage of the recovery to build up a work for themselves. They did their work under the cloak of the recovery's work.

From 1984 to 1986 I called for urgent meetings of all the elders and co-workers at least four times. In my opening word I told them that I called them to these meetings because I realized that among us there were strong signs that division would come in. These messages are now in Books 1 through 8 of a series entitled *Elders' Training*. I indicated that some of the brothers were apparently working for the recovery, but actually they were not. They were taking advantage of the recovery to work out their kind of work. They were doing their work within the work of the Lord's recovery. But I warned them. I said, "According to what I saw with Brother Nee and according to what I have experienced in my period of ministry, no one would be benefited by doing such a work. You will only damage yourself, terminate yourself, and deaden the weaker saints in the recovery."

Divisions have come in among us just because of ambition. Recently, I have studied 1 and 2 Kings. Among the many kings, probably only David had no aspiration or intention to build up his little empire. But besides him many had the intention to build up their own empire, their monarchy.

Brother Nee ministered on the Body of Christ again and again, but eventually, turmoil arose that forced him to stop his ministry. He himself stopped, telling us he would not minister, and this took place for six years. In 1948 his ministry was brought back and resumed through the recovery among us. We have published a two-volume set entitled *Messages Given during the Resumption of Watchman Nee's Ministry*. I would encourage you to read these messages. In one of these messages Brother Nee told us that some of the local churches had been taken by the so-called elders to make their churches "native" monarchies, little empires. This is not a church in the fellowship of the Body but just a little church in their own locality.

It is true to say that according to the Bible, the local churches are distinct from one another to a certain degree, but only in their business affairs, not in the spiritual testimony of Jesus. During the recent rebellion some misused Brother Nee's book *The Normal Christian Church Life* to say that the local churches are independent. After the apostles set up the church and appoint the elders, the apostles should take their hands off the church and leave the church to the elders. Further, the elders are the authority of that church. When I heard this, I referred the saints to another book by Brother Nee entitled *Church Affairs*. Brother Nee said there that after the apostles set up the elders, they have to stay with the elders to teach them, instruct them, and train them in how to take care of the church.

In this chapter I have fellowshipped concerning these negative things because I realize that many saints today in the recovery are not aware of the mistakes that crept into the recovery. They may consider that the recovery is for the recovery of the local churches. I say yes with a but. Yes, Brother Nee did minister on the local churches, but he went on from the local churches to the Body of Christ. The local churches are too much in the expression of physical things. You have to arrange the elders and set up the deacons to take care of so many outward affairs. But with the Body of Christ there are no physical things. The local churches are nearly ninety percent physical, but they should be for something spiritual, and this spiritual thing is the Body of Christ.

THE CORPORATE LIVING
BY THE PERFECTED GOD-MEN

Now, what is the reality of the Body of Christ? In brief, the reality of the Body of Christ is a kind of corporate living, not a living by any individual. This corporate living is the aggregate of many saints who have been redeemed, regenerated, sanctified, and transformed by the processed and consummated God within them. By this indwelling consummated God, these redeemed saints have been made actual God-men.

In regeneration a person is made a God-man, but he is not a matured God-man. When some babes are born, they are so small and weak that they have to be put in an incubator. But after much growth these little ones can become tall and husky. We have been regenerated, but many of us are still like these little babes. We need to be nourished and perfected so that we can grow in life and become mature. The procedure in the church work is to beget, to nourish, and then to teach and perfect so that the saints may be mature to be built in the local churches for the building up of the Body of Christ. Thank the Lord that in His recovery a number of seeking ones have been perfected.

We know that God became a man to be a God-man. That little Jesus in the manger was a God-man, but who could realize this? He lived not only a life of man but also a life of God. Thus, His life was a life of a God-man. He appeared to His disciples and to the people as a genuine man. Many who heard Him were astounded and said, "Where did this man get these things? And what is this wisdom given to this man, and how is it that such works of power take place through His hands? Is not this the carpenter, the son of Mary, and brother of James and Joses and Judas and Simon? And are not His sisters here with us?" (Mark 6:2-3). They wondered how a man could do these things, displaying the top virtues among mankind.

Who is He? He is God becoming a man, a real man. Yet this man would not live by Himself, by His own human life. Rather, He rejected His human life. He denied Himself. He lived as a man by another life, by the life of God. He told us that whatever He did and whatever He spoke were not of Himself but of the Father who sent Him (John 14:10, 24). He was a real man living there, yet He was dying to His natural life. He was dying to live, dying to His natural man to live by God's life. That dying to His natural life is the cross, and His living by the divine life is in resurrection.

For thirty-three and a half years this God-man, Jesus, was

a genuine man, but He lived not by man's life but by God's life. To live such a life He had to be crucified. The crucifixion mentioned in the New Testament transpired on the wooden cross on Mount Calvary. But you have to realize that before Christ was there in the physical crucifixion, He was being crucified every day for thirty-three and a half years. Was not Jesus a human being, a genuine man? Yes. But He did not live by that genuine man. Instead, He kept that genuine man on the cross. Then, in the sense of resurrection, He lived God's life. God's life with all its attributes was lived within this God-man Jesus and expressed as this God-man's virtues.

Such a life was there originally just in an individual man, Jesus Christ. But this life has now been repeated, reproduced, in many men who have been redeemed and regenerated and who now possess the divine life within them. All of them have been nourished, sanctified, transformed, and perfected not just to be matured Christians but to be God-men. The reality of the Body of Christ is the corporate living by the perfected God-men, who are genuine men but are not living by their life but by the life of the processed God, whose attributes have been expressed through their virtues.

After my thirty-two years of ministry in the United States, I have the assurance that a number of you have been perfected. What is it to be perfected? It is to be matured by continually exercising to reject the self and live by another life. This is according to what Paul says: "I am crucified with Christ; and it is no longer I who live, but it is Christ who lives in me" (Gal. 2:20a). Paul lived by dying to live. He was dying to his natural man and living by his new man with the divine life. So he said that by the bountiful supply of the Spirit of Jesus Christ, he lived and magnified Christ (Phil. 1:19-21a).

We should not live by ourselves. According to God's design in His economy, we were already put on the cross. We should not call ourselves back off the cross. To remain on the cross is to bear the cross and be under the cross. I have been crucified. There is no more I. I am finished. I am through. But there is a new man with me. That is the resurrected God-created man uplifted with God's divinity in him. That man is actually God Himself. Now I live by that man. But if I do not practice to keep my old man on the cross, I can never live the new man. This is why in the first chapter of Philippians, Paul tells us he lived such a life by the bountiful supply of the Spirit of Jesus Christ.

A CORPORATE LIVING OF THE CONFORMITY TO THE DEATH OF CHRIST THROUGH THE POWER OF THE RESURRECTION OF CHRIST

In Philippians 3 Paul says that he lived a life conformed to the death of Christ (v. 10). The death of Christ is a mold, and Paul put himself into that death-mold to be conformed there. On this man, Paul, all men could see the mark and the image of the cross (Gal. 6:14, 17—see footnote 17[1], Recovery Version). His old life was conformed to the image of the death of Christ by the power of Christ's resurrection. The power of resurrection strengthened him to live the life of a God-man. The Lord expects that many of us would be such ones.

I do believe that among us there should be some like this, maybe not constantly but at least instantly like this. I can testify to you that I am like this. I dare not say constantly but at least instantly. Many times when I was trying to talk to my wife, something within said, "This is not from your spirit. This is from your old man." Right away I stopped. Sometimes I would go to her, and then right away I returned. This is because my going was by my natural man. While I was doing that, something within turned me. That was the very life-giving Spirit, the pneumatic Christ. The processed Triune God turned me, and that was in resurrection. Such a corporate living is the reality of the Body of Christ, dear saints. This is a corporate living of the conformity to the death of Christ through the power of the resurrection of Christ.

THE MINGLING LIVING, IN THE ETERNAL UNION, OF THE REGENERATED, TRANSFORMED, AND GLORIFIED TRIPARTITE GOD-MEN WITH THE TRIUNE GOD IN THE RESURRECTION OF CHRIST

The reality of the Body of Christ is not just a corporate living but a mingling living. If we use the word *mingled,* this means that this living is consummated, completed. Instead, we use the word *mingling* because this living is not completed; it is still going on. It is the mingling living in the eternal union of the regenerated, transformed, glorified tripartite God-men with the Triune God in the resurrection of Christ. This Triune God is the very pneumatic Christ as the embodiment of the processed and consummated Triune God, who is the all-inclusive Spirit as the reality of the pneumatic Christ and as the consummation of the processed Triune God. Such a mingling living is in the resurrection of Christ, and the reality of this resurrection is the Spirit. This resurrection imparts the consummated God and releases the death-overcoming life into the believers.

CONSUMMATING ULTIMATELY
IN THE NEW JERUSALEM

Dear saints, such a mingling living is the reality of the Body of Christ. If among us there is, if not in full at least in part, such a living, the reality of the Body of Christ is among us. This is the high peak of the recovery in the local churches like Mount Zion in the city of Jerusalem. Such a mingling living as the reality of the Body of Christ will consummate ultimately in the New Jerusalem in the new heaven and new earth as God's increase and expression for eternity.

Anyone who lives such a mingling life would never be a trouble to anyone. They have been delivered out of themselves and have been transformed and perfected. They would not despise or condemn anyone, nor would they be bothered by others. They would not have anything to do with dissension, rebellion, or division. Instead, they would be here in the recovery as the high peak, Mount Zion, in Jerusalem.

CHAPTER FIVE

THE REALITY OF THE BODY OF CHRIST

(2)

OUTLINE

  I. The corporate living by the perfected God-men, who are genuine men but are not living by their life but by the life of the processed God, whose attributes have been expressed through their virtues.

 II. A corporate living of the conformity to the death of Christ through the power of the resurrection of Christ—Phil. 3:10.

III. The mingling living, in the eternal union, of the regenerated, transformed, and glorified tripartite God-men with the Triune God (who is the pneumatic Christ as the embodiment of the processed and consummated Triune God, who is the all-inclusive Spirit as the reality of the pneumatic Christ and the consummation of the processed Triune God) in the resurrection of Christ, of which the life-giving Spirit is the reality and which imparts the consummated God and releases the death-overcoming life into the believers.

 IV. Consummating ultimately in the New Jerusalem in the new heaven and new earth as God's increase and expression for eternity.

The crucial part of our fellowship in the previous chapter still remains here as a burden. In this chapter we want to complete our fellowship on the reality of the Body of Christ.

I thank the Lord that in the last days He has unveiled to us the highest peak of His revelation in His holy Word concerning God's eternal economy. The blending conference is to bring us to reach this highest peak. To do this I still have a burden which is very, very crucial.

THE TRIUNE GOD'S INDWELLING WITHIN US

Although in this point what I am going to fellowship with you, doctrinally speaking, is quite common, it has not been practiced among us very much. This point is the Triune God's indwelling within us. Romans 8 says that the indwelling Spirit ministers life into our mortal being (v. 11). There the word *indwells* is strongly stressed. Actually, the Lord's word while He was on earth referred to this already. In John 14:17-20 the Lord told us that by the Spirit of reality coming into us the Lord would live. Where would He live? He would live in us. And who is He? He is not just Jesus Christ but the Spirit of reality. So no doubt, this means that when the Spirit of reality comes, the Lord Himself would dwell in us in order to live in us. He said, "Because I live, you also shall live" (v. 19b). He lives and we live.

If you read this portion of the Word carefully, you can see that this is not a kind of individual living. This is a corporate living that we live with the Lord since He lives within us. We live together a corporate living. John 14:20 says, "In that day you will know that I am in My Father, and you in Me, and I in you." These three *in*s indicate a strong fact, which is very, very glorious. The eternal God, after His creation and after passing through the necessary processes, eventually became the Spirit of reality. As such a Spirit, He lives in us that we may live together with Him. So this living is a mingling. These three *in*s— I am in My Father, you in Me, and I in you—indicate not only a corporate living but also a mingling.

For us to reach the high peak of God's economy, that is, the reality of the Body of Christ, we must first see this divine indwelling within us. We may know this already, but we have not paid sufficient attention to it. In other words, I do not believe that anyone among us, including me, is constantly and instantly living with the indwelling Lord.

CHRIST BUILDING HIS HOME IN US

The apostle Paul tells us in the Epistles that Christ as the Spirit indwells us, and he goes on to tell us that He not only indwells us but also makes His home in our hearts (Eph. 3:17). To make a home is much more than to dwell. The Lord is not just dwelling within us. He is building His home in us. This means that this Indweller is dwelling in us in a very positive sense. While He dwells in us, He builds Himself as the very element into our being to build up a kind of wonderful constitution for Him to dwell in.

Many of us are familiar with Ephesians 3:17. I myself have put out many messages on Christ making His home in our hearts. But I do not believe that anyone among us, including me, has ever paid adequate attention to the fact that day after day the indwelling Christ is building, constituting, a structure in us for Him to dwell in as His home. I never was so impressed about this matter until the recent winter training on 1 and 2 Samuel.

The light on 2 Samuel 7:12-14 came to me while I was speaking. I did not have this light even when I wrote the outlines for the training. I would ask you to read the Life-study messages on this portion of the Word. David wanted to build a house, a temple, for God, but God stopped David. Instead, He told David that He would build Himself into David to be his seed, and this seed eventually would be born to be the Son of God. This reveals God building Himself into a human being to be a human seed. Eventually, this human seed would be born into divinity to be the firstborn Son of God, and this is confirmed by David's second Psalm: "You are My Son; / Today I have begotten You" (v. 7). God said this to David's seed. Then in Acts 13 Paul told us that this birth was Christ's resurrection (v. 33). Christ was begotten to be the firstborn Son of God with humanity uplifted to the divine standard in and by His resurrection.

In the life-study on Samuel, I pointed out two verses. One is Ephesians 3:17. Christ is now making His home in us. He is building Himself into our being to be a kind of structure for

Him to dwell in. Another verse is John 14:23. The Lord said, "If anyone loves Me...We [My Father and I] will come to him and make an abode with him." To make an abode is to build a house, which is the Father's house. John 14:2 says that in the Father's house there are many abodes. The Lord makes an abode with us in this age, the age of the church, for God to build up a house for Himself and for us as well.

Now we need to consider what this house is. I believe that since the history of the church began, no one has ever touched this matter thoroughly. Today the Lord has shown this to us. What is the age of the church? This is the age of God's divine building. Paul says in 1 Corinthians 3:9 that we are God's farm to grow Christ. To grow Christ is to produce some element for God to build up His building in this age. So the following words of verse 9 say, "You are...God's building."

While Paul spoke this, he was doing the building. He said that he had laid the unique foundation, that is, Jesus Christ (vv. 10-11). Now we, including Paul, are building upon this foundation. But we must be careful about what kind of material we build with. There are two categories of material. One category is wood, grass, and stubble. These are the earthen things. The second category is gold, silver, and precious stones (v. 12). Gold, silver, and precious stones are found in the earth, but they are the earthen things that have been transformed to be the very material with the divine element with which we build the church, that is, the Body of Christ.

Many of you are co-workers, and you do not know what a heavy burden I have for you all. Since the Lord has opened my eyes, I cannot deny that I have seen something. But I am very concerned about whether you have seen this or not. Are you building the so-called church you are in with wood, grass, and stubble? Paul says that if you do this, you mar the temple of God (v. 17—see footnote 1, Recovery Version). Mar is the opposite of beautify. To mar is to defile, ruin, or corrupt. To try to build up the church with wood, grass, and stubble is to mar the church.

Without your work, the church as the temple of God would remain just as it is. But after you come, you add some work into the church where you are, and this work is of wood, grass, and stubble. This means that the intrinsic element of your work is the natural man and the flesh, with something of the evil nature inside. In the outward element, you may help people to preach the gospel and do other things, but what you have done is full of the flesh, the natural man, and the earthly things. This kind of work is to mar God's building today.

The Lord dwells in us to build Himself into our being and to build us into His being. He builds the redeemed, uplifted man in Christ's resurrection into divinity. Christ builds this man into Himself. In John 15 the Lord said, "Abide in Me and I in you" (v. 4). This implies building. If we abide in Christ, we build ourselves into Christ, or we may say we are built into Christ. While Christ abides in us, He is building Himself into our being. Eventually, this is a mutual abiding, mutual dwelling, and mutual building.

The New Testament stresses this to the uttermost. The Spirit as the pneumatic Christ, the processed and consummated Triune God, is building Himself into us and building us into Him. Ephesians 4 tells us clearly that there is one Body, one Spirit, one Lord, and one God and Father of all (vv. 4-6). The redeemed ones who were born of the Spirit to be the children of the Father are the very Body of Christ, and the Spirit, the Lord, and the Father are built within them. All three of the Divine Trinity have been built into the redeemed and regenerated believers. We must see this.

A MUTUAL LIVING WITH CHRIST WHO LIVES IN US

We need to live a life with Christ who lives in us, to have a mutual abiding, a mutual building, a mutual living. Paul says, "I am crucified with Christ; and it is no longer I who live, but it is Christ who lives in me." Yet Paul goes on to say, "And the life which I now live in the flesh I live in faith, the faith of the Son of God" (Gal. 2:20). Paul lived by the faith of Christ. The faith of Christ is nothing less than Christ Himself. Christ is the Author and the Finisher of our faith (Heb. 12:2). For Paul to live by the faith of Christ meant that he lived by Christ. Christ lived in him, and he lived by Christ. He did this by the bountiful supply, not of the Spirit of God but of the Spirit of Jesus Christ, who became incarnated, passed through human living, died on the cross, and was resurrected. Such a One today is the bountiful Spirit. It is by this bountiful Spirit with His bountiful supply that Paul lived Christ and magnified Christ (Phil. 1:19-21a). He also said that he was pursuing after Christ, desiring to be conformed to His death by realizing the power of His resurrection (3:10).

How could we live with Christ? Not by ourselves but by the bountiful supply of the Spirit of Jesus Christ and by being conformed to His death through the power of His resurrection. I can live a life that is seemingly a human life, but not by my natural life. My natural life is left on the cross, and my daily life is being conformed to the image of Christ's death. Christ's death is a mold, and my living is a piece of dough put into the mold to be conformed to the image of the mold. Day by day I am dying to live. I am dying by the cross to live in the power of resurrection.

Paul says that such a person has his being in this marvelous Spirit and does everything according to such a Spirit (Gal. 5:16, 25; Rom. 8:4). David was a man according to God's heart, but that is far away from what we have. We are God-men who are doing things and having our being not only according to God's heart but also according to the Spirit who has been processed and consummated through death and resurrection. We need to check whether or not we are doing everything in the Spirit and having our being according to such a Spirit.

THE REALITY OF THE BODY OF CHRIST CONSUMMATING IN THE NEW JERUSALEM

The reality of the Body of Christ is the aggregate, the totality, of such a living by a group of God-men. This kind of a living, which is the reality of the Body of Christ, will close this age, the age of the church, and will bring Christ back to take, possess, and rule over this earth with these God-men in the kingdom age. They were perfected, completed, and consummated in the church age. So in the next age, the kingdom age, they will reign with Christ for a thousand years (Rev. 20:4-6).

The many believers who were not perfected and matured in the church age will be perfected and matured in the kingdom age by God's disciplinary dealing. God has a way. Not one believer can participate in the New Jerusalem without being perfected and matured. So in the thousand years of the kingdom age, God will exercise His sovereignty to discipline these dear ones, to deal with them in many ways, in order that He could perfect them to make them mature. At the end of the thousand years they will be ready to join the ones who were matured earlier in participating in the New Jerusalem.

Today in the church age, the God-men who were perfected and matured are Zion, the overcomers, the vital groups within the churches. But in the new heaven and new earth there will be no more Zion, only Jerusalem, because all the unqualified saints will have been qualified to be Zion. In other words, the entire New Jerusalem will become Zion. What is Zion? Zion is the very spot where God is, that is, the Holy of Holies. In Revelation 21 there is a sign signifying that the New Jerusalem will be the Holy of Holies. Its dimensions are the dimensions of a cube, twelve thousand stadia long, twelve thousand stadia wide, and twelve thousand stadia high (v. 16). That is the Holy of Holies, because the Holy of Holies in the Old Testament in both the tabernacle and the temple was a cube, equal in length, breadth, and height (Exo. 26:2-8; 1 Kings 6:20).

By that time all the God-redeemed people will be transformed, not only to be the same as God in life and nature but also to be the same in God's appearance. Revelation 4 tells us that God looks like jasper (v. 3). Then Revelation 21 says that the entire New Jerusalem has the appearance of jasper (v. 11). Thus, God's redeemed people have become absolutely the very God in life, in nature, and in appearance but not in His Godhead.

We all have to endeavor to reach this high peak. If you think it is too hard to reach this high peak and that the price to pay is too high, be prepared. In the next age the price will be higher. Sooner or later, you have to be made God, either in the church age or in the coming kingdom age. All of God's redeemed people will eventually become gods as the very God in life, in nature, and in appearance but not in the Godhead. The New Jerusalem is the God-men who have been transformed, glorified, and mingled with the processed and consummated Triune God. The holy city will be a mingling to be God's increase and expression for eternity. We will enjoy and participate in this divine mingling for eternity.

We surely need to be desperate to pray at any cost and to pay the cost just as the apostle Paul did. We should not have the attitude that we are safe in the Lord because we have sacrificed our future and do not love the world. That is not adequate. You must know the intrinsic scene of all the spiritual things. God's intention is to make Himself man that man may become Him. Then He and man will be united and mingled together to live a corporate life. Eventually, this holy city, Jerusalem, is the aggregate of all the visions and revelations. It is a constitution of the Triune God with the tripartite man. This constitution, the New Jerusalem, will be a pair of lovers in eternity. This pair of lovers are men and God as well. They have become a kind of mutual abode in divinity and humanity. In this humanity, the glory of God will be expressed, manifested, to the uttermost, full of brightness, full of splendor, and full of glory.

What shall we do in the light of this revelation? There is no other way to reach this high peak except by praying. It is more than evident that Jerusalem is here as a big realm of Christians, but where is Zion, the overcomers? In the book of Revelation what the Lord wants and what the Lord will build up is Zion, the overcomers. The overcomers are the very Zion, where God is. This is the intrinsic reality of the spiritual revelation in the holy Word of God. We have to realize what the Lord's recovery is. The Lord's recovery is to build up Zion. Paul's writings unveil this to the uttermost, but not many saw this in the past.

I do ask you to reverently consider this matter. Paul said that all run in the race, but only one receives the prize. Then he said that we should run in such a way to receive the reward (1 Cor. 9:24). At the end of Paul's life he said that he had fought the good fight, finished the course, and kept the faith. He testified that there was a crown of righteousness prepared for him (2 Tim. 4:7-8). I hope that when we end this life, we could say that we have done the same thing. Otherwise, we will be a dropout in the school of the church life. But the Lord will still pick us up in the school of the kingdom age. If we are not perfected in this age, the Lord will spend one thousand years to perfect us. The Lord would even use the second death, which is the fire of the lake of fire, to discipline us (Rev. 2:11). I am thankful to the

Lord for the spreading of His recovery, but on the other hand, in these few years my heart is very heavy not only concerning you but also concerning myself.

ABOUT THE AUTHOR

Witness Lee was born in 1905 in northern China and raised in a Christian family. At age nineteen he was fully captured for Christ and immediately consecrated himself to preach the gospel for the rest of his life. Early in his service, he met Watchman Nee, a renowned preacher, teacher, and writer. Witness Lee labored together with Watchman Nee under his direction. In 1934 Watchman Nee entrusted Witness Lee with the responsibility for his publication operation, called the Shanghai Gospel Book Room.

Prior to the Communist takeover in 1949, Witness Lee was sent by Watchman Nee and his other co-workers to Taiwan to ensure that the things delivered to them by the Lord would not be lost. Watchman Nee instructed Witness Lee to continue the former's publishing operation abroad as the Taiwan Gospel Book Room, which has been publicly recognized as the publisher of Watchman Nee's works outside China. Witness Lee's work in Taiwan manifested the Lord's abundant blessing. From a mere three hundred fifty believers, newly fled from the mainland, the churches in Taiwan grew to twenty thousand believers in five years.

In 1962 Witness Lee felt led of the Lord to move to the United States, and he began to minister in Los Angeles in December of that year. During his thirty-five years of service throughout the United States, he ministered in weekly meetings, weekend conferences, and weeklong trainings, delivering several thousand spoken messages. His speaking has since been published, and many of his books have been translated into numerous languages. He gave his last public conference in February 1997 at the age of ninety-one and went to be with the Lord, whom he loved and served, on June 9, 1997. Witness Lee leaves behind a prolific presentation of the truth in the Bible. His major work, *Life-study of the Bible*, the fruit of his labor from 1974 to 1995, comprises over twenty-five thousand pages of commentary on every book of the Bible from the perspective of the believers' enjoyment and experience of God's divine life in Christ through the Holy Spirit. In addition, *The Collected Works of Witness Lee* contains over one hundred thirty volumes (over seventy-five thousand pages) of his other ministry from 1932 to 1997. Witness Lee was also the chief editor of a new translation of the New Testament into Chinese called the Recovery Version, and he directed the translation of the English New Testament Recovery Version. The Recovery Version also appears in over twenty-five other languages. In the Recovery Version he provided an extensive body of footnotes, outlines, and spiritual cross references. A radio broadcast of his messages can be heard on Christian radio stations in the United States and Europe. In 1965 Witness Lee founded Living Stream Ministry, a non-profit corporation, located in Anaheim, California, which publishes his and Watchman Nee's ministry.

Witness Lee's ministry emphasizes the experience of Christ as life and the practical oneness of the believers as the Body of Christ. Stressing the importance of attending to both of these matters, he led the churches under his care to grow in Christian life and function. He was unbending in his conviction that God's goal is not narrow sectarianism but the universal Body of Christ. In time, believers everywhere began to meet simply as the church in their localities in response to this conviction. Through his ministry hundreds of local churches have been raised up throughout the earth.